W9-AST-134

Follow
the
Butterfly
Stream

Follow the Butterfly

Stream

text and photographs by
Lorenz Boyd

Abingdon Press
Nashville   New York

Follow the Butterfly Stream
Text and photographs by Lorenz Boyd

ISBN 0-687-13242-8
Library of Congress Catalog Card Number: 79-147302

Printed in the United States of America

For

Lisbeth and Lanette

In the Great Smoky Mountains we
have followed often the course of the waters
flowing downward through wooded hills to
become Roaring Fork and, then, Little Pigeon River.
Wherever we were along its course,
my daughters called it "the butterfly stream."

So I borrow their name for it and dedicate this
to Lisbeth and Lanette
and the memories of our wonder
along the butterfly stream.

The woods are made for
the hunters of dreams,

The brooks for the fishers of song;

To the hunters who hunt for
the gunless game

The streams and the woods belong.

—SAM WALTER FOSS

Spring has come to the mountains of
the butterfly stream. Snow still lingers
along the highest ridges. But bear have begun to
leave their dens after a long winter hibernation,
to move down toward the lower forests where they will
spend summer hunting and fishing
along the butterfly stream.

And you? Well, there are things for you to find
if you follow the butterfly stream.
Come down from the snowy peaks where wind
whistles chilly tunes in your ears;
come down into the dense green forests where mist and rain
have spread a splendid carpet for wanderers.

On the thick tops of hemlock, birch, beech,
and tulip trees sunlight can dance, but it seldom finds
room to break through to touch the forest floor.
There in the cool dampness moss, liverwort, and
lichen blanket the rocks and the fallen trees.

Giant white blossoms dot thickets of rosebay rhododendron.
Mushrooms make orange and red splashes
on the forest floor and on rotting stumps.
Indian pipe, or ghost plant, eerily struggles upward.

If you listen, listen very carefully, you will hear it.
A pattering, trickling, splashing sound. Move toward the
sound and you find a little stream flowing over and around
rocks, under toppled trees, and through green thickets.

Cup your hands and taste the cool, clear water—
the pure water where the butterfly stream is
young and fresh from mountain springs.

Then, follow the butterfly stream.
Climb over or duck under trees that have fallen
across the meandering little stream. Other brooks
and streams flow into it, and suddenly it is stronger.
Now it hurries to drop down through the mountains,
and begins to roar impatiently at the rocks
in its way. It dashes and splashes around
the rocks, making white cascades.

If you look up one of the brooks that flow into the butterfly stream, you see a ridge where many tiny streams have joined to make a waterfall. Each of the rivulets has cut its own course over the ledge. They flow, trickle, or drip over the rock. It is slate—soft when compared to many kinds of rock. Each drop of flowing or dripping water is cutting the rock away and thousands of years from now they may have cut a new forest canyon. Today's small streams unite in the waterfall to pour as one into the turbulent butterfly stream.

Proud Cherokee once lived in the forest of the
butterfly stream. They hunted deer that came to drink
at the stream and bear that fished in the white cascades.

If you stop to rest and let your heart look and listen, you can
almost see the Cherokee children chasing the
yellow-winged tiger swallowtails flying
along the banks, and you can almost hear
the children shouting excitedly, "KAMama! KAMama!"
which is the Cherokee word for butterfly.

Flashing yellow wings of the male tiger swallowtail are seen
everywhere along the butterfly stream as the males search for mates.
The female tiger finds a shady, bare spot along the stream.

There she spreads her wings for the male
to see her shining color. He lands beside
her and their courtship begins.
Later she will lay eggs on the leaves of tulip trees
or wild cherry, food plants of the caterpillars
that will hatch from the eggs.

Often the female tiger is yellow like the male,
but larger. Along the butterfly stream
the female tiger is found also in a dark form,
with dark wings and shining white and orange spots.
Perhaps this different coloring protects her for she
then looks much like another swallowtail, the pipe-vine,
also found along the butterfly stream. Birds do
not eat the pipe-vine swallowtail. They avoid it.

The female pipe-vine swallowtail also attracts her
mate by finding an open place along the banks of the butterfly
stream, spreading her wings to reveal her

blue color and the white crescents along
her lower wing tips. The male's coloring is much the same, but
he is smaller.

Soon after mating the female pipe-vine swallowtail flits along
the banks of the stream, patting the leaves of plants.
She is tasting the leaves, for butterflies taste with
their feet. At last she finds the leaf she
is looking for—pipe vine, the food plant of the
caterpillars that become pipe-vine swallowtails.
Now she tucks under the green, heart-shaped leaf of the
pipe vine and lays several golden eggs. When the
caterpillars hatch, there will be pipe vine to feast on.
Perhaps something in the pipe vine leaves gives an
alarming taste to the butterflies which develop from the
caterpillars, happily protecting them from hungry birds.

You come upon a giant boulder in the forest
along the butterfly stream. How did the boulder get there?
For every forest riddle there is an answer. The forest
was not made by a haphazard hand. Each part of the
puzzle fits together with other parts.

At the time of the Ice Age, great glaciers,
mighty rivers of slowly flowing ice, came down from
the north carrying huge masses of boulders with them.
But the glaciers never reached the land of the butterfly
stream. Nevertheless, the bitter cold did. Water which
had seeped into the rocks of the mountains froze,
expanded and tore apart the surface.
Boulders broke loose and tumbled down until they
crashed to a stop against ancient trees.

The boulder holds the answer to some forest riddles.
It can show you how the forest soil began.
Lichen growing on the rock produces acid which breaks down
the rock; and small particles of rock mixed with
decayed lichen was the beginning of the soil.
Then other plants grew, died and decayed,
making the soil thicker and richer. Each rotting tree
fallen in the forest is adding soil even now.
You can see that leaves and other debris have fallen on
top of the boulder and have provided enough soil for
leafy plants to grow there.

Trees around the boulder are those that like high, shady places. Their seeds sprout and grow in shade and thrive in shallow, moist soil. They like the cool climate here, as do moss, mushrooms, millipedes, slugs, and tree snails.

But if you follow the butterfly stream farther down the mountains, both the stream and the forest change. Now there appear trees that do not grow well in the shade of high places—oak, maple, and sugar maple. The butterfly stream is calmer here, and deeper. Its banks and bottom are made with smooth, rounded rocks and pebbles. Along the banks splotches of brilliant wild flowers appear, like the orange butterfly weed.

tickweed

Turk's-cap lily

Flowers grow in
every sun-filled open space.

black-eyed Susan

wild geranium

Indian pipe (ghost plant)

St.-John's-wort

Swallowtails still
are found along the
butterfly stream,
but now they
have the company
of woodland
and grassland
butterflies—
the blues,
buckeyes,
hairstreaks,
anglewings,
sulphurs,
metalmarks, and
coppers. If you sit
on the bank of the
butterfly stream,
you can watch
a whole parade
of butterflies—
all kinds,
shapes, sizes,
and colors.

common sulphur

Eastern tailed blue

a tortoise shell

a crescent

little metalmark

The seemingly fearless little American copper
hovers on black and copper-colored wings at
a daisy, feasting. Like all butterflies, its
mouth is actually a long tube called a proboscis.
When not in use the tube curls up,
out of sight; but when the butterfly feeds,
the tube extends like a soda straw into the heart of
the flower to suck sweet nectar.

The little copper has a good device for protection.
He attacks. He flies at birds, larger butterflies,
and even at raccoons as if he had a secret weapon.
He doesn't have any weapon at all. His fierce attack, however,
is often enough to cause a hungry bird to fly
away and look elsewhere for a meal.

Every spring and summer day in grassy spaces along
the butterfly stream a marvelous event begins.
It happens over and over.
A caterpillar climbs out on a twig or a blade of grass
and makes a sticky silk pad to hold it there. It hangs
from the twig for a few days until something amazing happens.
The skin breaks open and the pupa living inside
the caterpillar appears. It is brown and soft and moist.
It squirms and twists until
the caterpillar skin falls to the ground.

The air dries and hardens the outside of the pupa.
For many days it hangs there and seems to become drier and
harder. Then one morning it is dark and moist again.

life cycle of the buckeye

It jerks on the twig but it does
not fall from the silk pad. Suddenly the
shell splits, and a butterfly with
limp, wet wings climbs out and clings to the twig.

The butterfly pumps fluid from its body into the
veins of its wings and the wings become straight.
It waits for the wings to dry, and from time to
time it waves them to hurry the drying.

life cycle of the buckeye

treehopper

Finally the wings are dry, and the butterfly joins others in the meadow beside the stream.

How quiet the butterfly stream seems in the heart of summer. In the woods around it, prowling the leaves and branches, are tiny creatures with shapes stranger than the dinosaurs that lived here millions of years ago. Some of the strangest shapes belong to treehoppers, resembling in both shape and color budding leaves, thorns, and dead leaves.

Dragonflies and damselflies hunt on the wing over the butterfly stream. Damselflies are usually smaller and slimmer than dragonflies, but it is hard to tell the difference when they are in flight or hovering near the stream.

But there's no problem when they rest, for dragonflies rest with their wings spread, damselflies rest with their wings closed.

Millions of years ago there were dragonflies here with wings two and a half feet long, but that was before there were birds. Today the dragonflies of the butterfly stream have wings only three or four inches long, but they are quick and have perhaps the best eyesight of all insects. They can spot a flying gnat nearly twenty feet away.

damselfly

dragonflies

In the gentle stream minnows and crayfish peep out at you and
then dart out of sight under rocks and pebbles.
Water striders skim over the surface and make ripples.

But the best ripple-makers are raindrops. First one,
then another and another, until the shower ruffles
the stream and patters on the dry leaves and brush in the woods.

After the rain the air is fresh and the stream
becomes peaceful again. In the returning sun,
water sparkles like happy teardrops on the petals of flowers.

Finally the day will arrive when the breeze is chilled
and the first golden leaf sails easily
through the air and drops softly on the butterfly stream.
Other leaves will follow as the woods turn red and gold.

Bear eat hungrily as they head back up to the
high country and their dens. Chattering squirrels
busily store nuts in their nests. Walkingstick insects
mate, and the female drops over a hundred eggs
on the ground, not to hatch until the spring.

Butterflies have different ways to live through
winter or to assure more of their kind next spring.
Some migrate far to the south where they hibernate.
Some cling to leaves and hibernate near the butterfly stream.
Others spend the winter as caterpillars in loose
silk cocoons on leaves or twigs. Still others,
such as the swallowtails, become a rough brown pupa
on twigs, but the butterfly will not break out until spring.

So winter will come
to the butterfly stream,
bringing to mountain
forests a different
kind of beauty.
Trees will be bare.
Grass will be brown.
There will be no flowers.
Snow will fall, and ice
will form on the
edges of the stream.
Rhododendron leaves will
curl tightly and
point downward in the
bitter cold. But there
will be another spring,
when the butterflies
again will flash
their wings along the
roaring white
waters of
the butterfly stream.